This book belongs to:

_____

entrepreneur

Note to parents and educators:

Hello! Thank you for your interest in *Lull and His Ladybugs*. This is the first in a series of children's books that aim to empower kids to overcome life's challenges and shortcomings through innovative thinking. My entrepreneurial spirit emerged at a young age, stemming from an early awareness of my family's limited financial resources. My parents gave me the freedom to explore my ideas and interests no matter how crazy they may have sounded, and trust me, they were skeptical about a lot of them. Nonetheless, their belief in me encouraged me to think about and strive for things that were beyond what most 7-year-olds considered. Whether or not you want your child to grow up to become business people, there is great value in instilling a sense that they can find creative solutions to life's problems, and that ultimately they can accomplish anything they set their minds to, today and for the future.

Note to kids:

Hey hey hey! Are you excited about becoming an entrepreneur? It's OK if the word "entrepreneur" sounds funny or strange, it is a pretty hard word to say. It simply means having your own business and being your own boss. And it is easy to become an entrepreneur, no matter what age you are, whether you run a lemonade stand or trade ladybugs for other cool things like I did when I was your age. If you take anything from this book, know that you can turn any idea into a reality. Ask your parents or friends to help you, but do not let anyone stop *you* from trying.

Lull and His Ladybugs Copyright © 2010 by Lull Mengesha Publishing

Books published by Lull Mengesha Publishing are available at special discounts for bulk purchases globally by corporations, institutions, and other organizations. For more information, please contact Lull Mengesha Publishing at lullmengesha@gmail.com.

www.lullmengesha.com

Library of Congress Control Number: 2011906773

Mengesha, Lull
Lull and His Ladybugs/story and pictures by Lull Mengesha.
Series: Building an Entrepreneur

ISBN-13: 978-0-98357250-3
ISBN-10: 0-98357250-X
[Non-Fiction] I. Title. II. Series

May 2011

THIS IS A LULL MENGESHA BOOK PUBLISHED BY LULL MENGESHA PUBLISHING

Lull
and His
Ladybugs

"To those who
don't have much
the world is still
equally yours."

-Lull Mengesha Publishing

by Lull Mengesha

**Illustrated by
Nina Didenko
& Troy Tsuchikawa**

Lull Mengesha
PUBLISHING

Lull and his friends love to play games.

"Simon says...jump on one leg. Simon says...jump on two legs. Now put your hands on your stomach," laughs Lull.

"Lull, come inside!" Lull's mom yells from their apartment.

"Gotta go!" Lull yells back to his friends, running to his mom.

Lull gets to the apartment out of breath.

"Lull, I want you to go pick up potatoes from the neighbor. Bring him these onions to trade," Lull's mom says.

Lull doesn't understand why his mom doesn't just buy the potatoes at the store.

"Hi Lull!" the neighbor says.

"Mom needs potatoes, and she said you would trade her for onions," Lull replies. "Why don't you go to the store and buy onions instead?"

The neighbor takes a deep breath and explains, "Your mother and I don't have much money. So we trade to get what we want like when you and your friends trade for Silly Bands."

Lull understands. He and his friends trade Silly Bands. Once, he had one shaped like a dinosaur and his friend Aaron had one shaped like a star. So they traded without having to pay each other money.

The next day, Lull sits with his friends, Troy, Khasha, and Aaron, in the school cafeteria. For Lull and his friends, it's always the same old milk, same old trays, and same old table.

They watch the other kids who have sack lunches filled with peanut butter and jelly sandwiches, bite-sized candy bars, and pudding cups.

"Guys, look at those snacks!"
Khasha exclaims.

"It's not fair," says Aaron. Troy nods
in agreement.

"Let's ask our moms to buy them for us at
the store," suggests Lull. "It never hurts
to ask."

When Lull gets home from school, he asks his mom for a sack lunch.

"Lull, I love you, but we don't have the money and we don't have anything to trade for those kinds of things."

Lull can tell it bothers his mom. So he gives her a hug before going back outside.

"Guys, we have to find a way to get what we want, without money," says Lull, glancing from Khasha to Troy, and then at Aaron. "I wonder if the kids at school ever want stuff they don't have," he complains aloud.

Remembering how his mother got potatoes, Lull exclaims, "Guys, I figured it out! We are going to trade with our classmates for their homemade lunches!"

Khasha, Troy, and Aaron look doubtful.

"What are we going to trade?" asks Troy.

"I don't know yet," whispers Lull, "but we will have to look around and find things that our classmates want."

"I don't have anything to trade," Aaron replies.

"Well, let's look around the neighborhood and meet back with what we can find," says Lull.

After a few hours, Lull and his friends meet up again at the park. They have found a tennis ball, one shoe, and a plastic baseball bat.

"Well, I think the stuff we found is cool, but we need to find something they don't already have," says Lull.

He stares at the items they found, thinking of bite-sized candy bars.

From the swingset, Lull sees younger kids giggling in the distance as they try to catch ladybugs in their hands.

Lull remembers catching ladybugs when he was younger and putting them in a jar. His friends would beg him for the jar because it looked so cool.

Who wouldn't want a jar of ladybugs?

Suddenly, Lull knew what they would trade.
He yells out, "I've got it!"

Lull's friends stop playing and look at him.

"That's what we'll trade!" Lull exclaims.

"The little kids?" asks Khasha.

"No, silly. Ladybugs!" says Lull.

"Are you kidding? Why would they want bugs?" asks Troy.

"We used to have fun with them," Lull answers, "maybe the kids at school will like them, too."

Lull and his friends go get glass jars from their houses and meet back at the park, where the little kids are catching ladybugs. They help Lull and his friends fill the jars, too. As a reward, Lull lets the little kids take turns being Simon in Simon Says.

As a team, Lull, his friends, and the little kids collect four jars of ladybugs.

The next day, in the cafeteria, Lull and his friends sit at their table.

"Here goes nothing," says Lull, grabbing his backpack with the four jars of ladybugs inside. "I have been practicing asking the kids with homemade lunches to trade."

Lull walks over to the table of kids that eat sack lunches.

"You want to see something cool?" Lull asks. He feels stronger and bigger than normal, now that he has something valuable to trade.

"What could you have that I would want?" questions Jimmy, one of the sack lunch kids.

"Actually, never mind," replies Lull.
"I know the guys at the table over there
would rather see it." With his backpack,
Lull pretends to head to the next table.

"Come on Lull! Just show us what you
have!" whines Jimmy. The rest of the sack
lunch table looks eagerly at Lull.

"OK, guys. I'll show you," Lull says, happy with how badly the kids want to see what's in his backpack.

"So, who wants to make a trade?" Lull asks the eager faces around him.

All the kids at the table raise their hands and yell, "I do, I do!"

"Let's see what you guys have for lunch that I would be willing to trade for," says Lull.

The kids show their lunches to Lull, and are soon offering more and more for the prized ladybugs. Even Jimmy and the other sack lunch kids want to trade for a ladybug jar.

Lull trades the four jars of ladybugs for the best snacks: cookies, juice boxes, and crust-free sandwiches.

Lull takes the snacks he traded for back to his friends and puts them on the table.

"I can't believe this worked!" exclaims Troy.

"We're going to be millionaires!" says Aaron.

"I like the sound of that!" responds Lull.

Lull and his friends gather and trade ladybugs for the next few weeks, until the sack lunch kids move on to new video games and toys.

Lull is bothered that he can't keep trading ladybugs for lunch. After school one day, he says to his mom, "People don't want our ladybugs anymore."

"Oh well, I'll bet you'll think of something new that the kids will want," says Lull's mom, smiling knowingly.

Lull anxiously runs back to meet his friends,
"Hey guys, I have another idea!"

Activity Page

What do you want that you do not have?

_____

What could you trade?

_____

List people who you can trade with.

_____

_____

_____

Meet the Author

Lull Mengesha

Lull was born in Khartoum, Sudan to
Ethiopian parents. While still an infant,
his family moved to the United States,
settling in Bayview Heights - a lower-
income neighborhood in San Diego,
California. Lull gives all credit for his
business savvy to his surroundings
growing up - inspired by the creative
ways people made a living.

Lull is also the author of *The Only Black
Student*, which serves as a guide for
students of color navigating at the
collegiate level.

Meet the Illustrators

Nina Didenko

Nina studied art in Kramotosk City in Ukraine, Donetsk region. She has worked in digital illustration for six years and specializes in 2-D illustrations and cartoons. After pitting her work against other artists via social media, she received an overwhelming amount of praise, ultimately solidifying her participation on the *Ladybugs* project.

Troy Tsuchikawa

Troy hails as a business student from Seattle University, where he also studied his first love - graphic design. He maintains a full-time office job while engaging in more artistic endeavors on the side. Troy is also an avid supporter of entrepreneurship as he believes that nothing should stop you from attaining your dream.

Made in the USA
San Bernardino, CA
05 July 2017